help**me**
B E C O M E™

Becoming **Content** &
Overcoming **Complaining**™

REAL
mvpkids®

Cure Complaining™

SOPHIA DAY®

Written by Kayla Pearson   Illustrated by Timothy Zowada

WELCOME to the WORLD OF

mvpkids

Everything we create is with the intention of nurturing a child's character. Our mission is to equip parents, teachers and caregivers to engage with kids through inspiring entertainment.

nurture
LITERACY™

cultivate
MENTORSHIP™

inspire
CHARACTER®

expand
EDUCATION™

enrich
ENTERTAINMENT

May your childhood be filled with adventure, your days with hope and your learnings with wisdom, and may you continuously grow as an MVP Kid, preparing to lead a responsible, meaningful life.

— SOPHIA DAY

TABLE OF CONTENTS

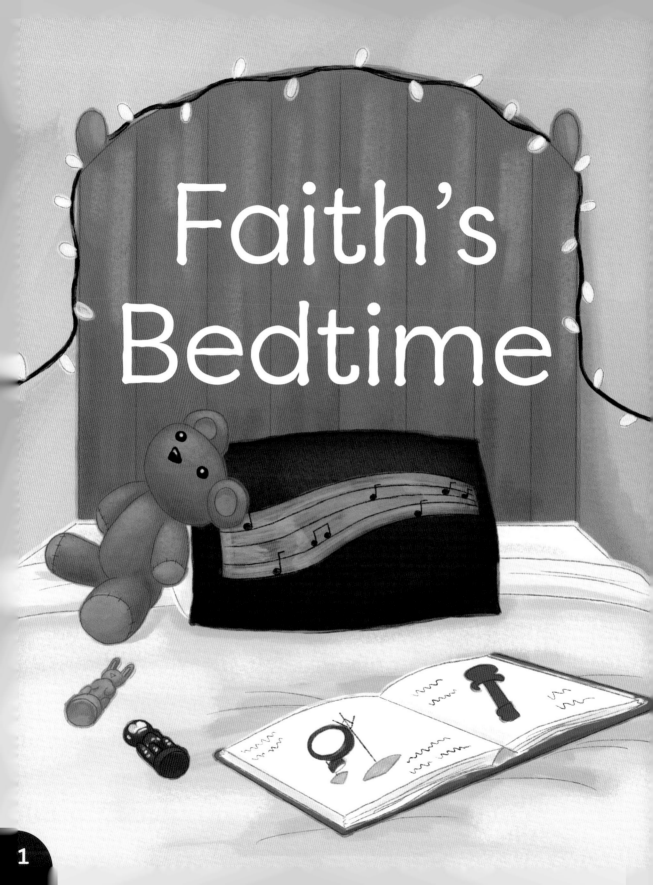

Faith's Bedtime

"Five minutes until bedtime!"

Faith's mom announced.

Faith sat at the table playing her favorite board game with her siblings.

Five minutes passed, and it was almost
Faith's turn again when she heard her mom say,
"Time for bed!"
"But Mom! Can we have five more minutes?"
asked Faith. She really hoped she could
finish the game.

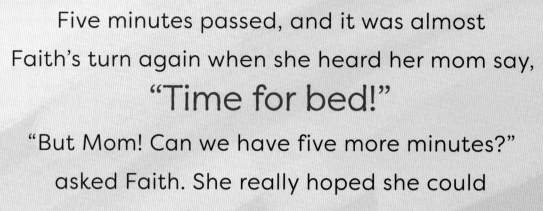

"Faith, I already gave you a five-minute warning. It's bedtime now. Please listen," her mom replied. "This isn't fair!" Faith complained as she started getting ready for bed.

Faith went to
the sink to brush
her teeth.
"I don't want
to use the mint
toothpaste,"
she complained.

Faith stomped
away and
started to put
on her PJs.
"I don't like
these PJs,"
she complained
again.

Faith went to the
bookshelf to pick
out a book.
"I've already read
all these books."

Faith laid down
in bed and
began to cry.
"This has been a
terrible day!"

Faith's mom came in to say good night, but saw
Faith was sick with the complaining virus.

"Faith, I'm sorry you couldn't have more time to play,
but getting enough sleep is important,"
said her mom.

"Did you notice how you caught the complaining virus when you became frustrated?" Faith's mom asked.

"Complaining virus?" Faith sat up.

"Yes, you started to complain about everything, even the things that you like. When we complain, our words and attitude may spread, even to people around you, just like a cold virus."

Faith thought about what her mom said.
She was right.

When she complained about the toothpaste, Malik didn't want to brush his teeth.

When she complained about her PJs, Harmony complained, too.

When she complained about the books, Ezekiel didn't want to read either.

"So **what do I do** when I catch the complaining virus?" asked Faith.

"Take a deep breath and try to relax for a moment. Think about why you're upset and what you can do to change it. For example, you were upset because you had to stop your game. Instead, you could start to look forward to what's next, like reading your favorite bedtime story."

"Oh! Do we still have time to read a book? I wanted to read a story to you tonight."

"Yes, honey. Because you obeyed even though you were upset, we can make time for a book tonight." She climbed in bed with her family.
The day didn't seem so terrible after all.

THINK & TALK ABOUT IT

Faith's Bedtime

Discuss the story...

1. Describe Faith's attitude at the beginning of the story.

2. What does Faith's mom mean by "complaining virus?"

3. Does Faith really have an illness?

4. What does Faith learn about herself in the story?

5. Describe how Faith changes from the beginning to the end of the story.

Learn more ways to cure complaining with
Faith's No Complaining Game on page 63!

For additional tips and reference information, visit **www.MVPkids.com**.

Discuss how to apply the story...

1. What are things you complain about often?

2. How do you feel when you complain?

3. How can your complaining affect those around you?

4. What can you do to cure the "complaining virus"?

5. What can you do to prevent getting the "complaining virus" from others?

FOR PARENTS & MENTORS: *Sometimes children may complain as a means of getting attention. Other times, complaining may have a deeper problem than what appears on the surface. Take time to identify the emotions your child is feeling that causes continual complaining. Expressing dissatisfaction can be a stress coping mechanism when dealing with anxiety. During the school-age years, children will begin to experience more mental, emotional and social stress. Allowing children to complain consistently is not good for them or their families. Finding the root problem and teaching them proper ways to handle stress will help them cope with problems more beneficially in the future.*

You may be able to identify certain triggers that can cause your child to spiral into a bad attitude. Transitions can often be one of those triggers. Having an established routine, like at bedtime, and giving time warnings can help make those transitions easier. When you stick to routines, your child will know what is expected and the consequences that will follow for disobedience.

Leo's Great Idea

Today was Leo's least favorite day of the week. *Chore day.* It was the day when each person in the family did extra chores to help around the house.

Dad mowed
the lawn.

Mom cleaned
the bathrooms.

Nonna* cleaned
the kitchen.

Junior picked up the
toys in the playroom.

Frankie vacuumed
the carpets.

*Nonna means
Grandmother in
Italian.

And Leo was stuck helping with the laundry.
Leo *did not* like doing laundry.

CHORES

- ☑ Mow Yard
- ☑ Clean Bathroom
- ☑ Clean Kitchen
- ☑ Pick Up Toys
- ☑ Vacuum
- ☑ Laundry

"Chore day is no fun and a lot of work," Leo complained to his mom.

"Leo, complaining isn't going to change things. We are a family, and we all need to do our part to take care of our home. If you don't like something, come up with a solution to make it better," challenged his mom.

"How can I make doing laundry better? *It's laundry,*" Leo kept thinking.

When he was finished eating, Leo placed his bowl in the sink and walked to his room.

There he saw a mound of clean laundry ready to be put away. Overwhelmed by the task, Leo felt like the laundry pile **grew until it towered** over him.

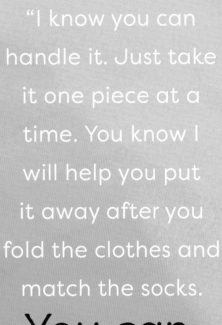

"I know you can handle it. Just take it one piece at a time. You know I will help you put it away after you fold the clothes and match the socks. **You can do it, Leo,"** his mom encouraged him.

Leo's mom left, and Leo looked at the pile once more. Then his cat knocked a fishing pole out of the closet. This gave Leo an idea!

"I can use the fishing pole to help put away the laundry!" said Leo.

He thought about making a game out of it.

He put shirts on hangers and hung them in the closet.

After matching socks, Leo opened the drawers with his fishing pole and tossed in the socks.

All he had left were his pants and shorts,
so he folded them and put them in the basket.
Then he hooked the basket and pulled it
across the room with the pole.

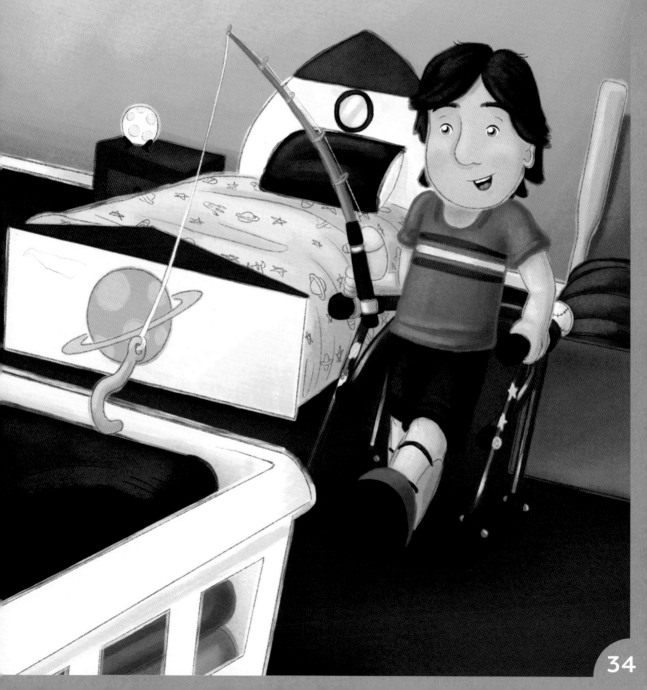

After placing the pants in
the drawer, he shouted,
"Yes! I'm finished!"

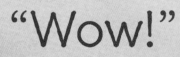

"Wow!"

His mom stopped
in his doorway.
"You finished
so quickly!"

"Yes! I listened to what you said. I came up with a solution to make laundry more fun. Then, I took it one piece at a time," answered Leo.

"I'm so
impressed, Leo.
Way to go!"
his mom said as she gave him a high-five.

THINK & ...TALK ABOUT IT

Leo's Great Idea

Discuss the story...

1. Describe Leo's attitude at the beginning of the story.

2. What is Leo's struggle in this story?

3. What other ways do you think Leo could have solved his problem?

4. How do you think Leo felt at the end of the story?

5. What do you think Leo will do the next time it is chore day?

Discuss how to apply the story...

1. What would happen if Leo's family didn't help clean the house?

2. What are some chores that you don't like?

3. Do you think complaining will solve your problems? Why or why not?

4. What can you do instead of complaining?

5. Sometimes you might feel overwhelmed or that a task is too big. What can you do to make the task feel smaller?

FOR PARENTS & MENTORS: *Complaining doesn't change a situation. Actions are the only way to create real, positive change. Teach children that complaining doesn't help by using those moments as opportunities to encourage problem solving. Instill confidence by assuring children that you believe they can figure out a solution. Encourage children to solve problems on their own, offering the least amount of assistance required based on age and situation. If the task seems too big, help them break it down into manageable parts. If the solution didn't turn out the way they intended, help them learn from their mistakes.*

*For additional tips and reference information, visit **www.MVPkids.com**.*

Julia's
New
Friend

Today Julia was going to the medical clinic to volunteer with her mom. She brought along some small toys to keep herself busy.

On their way, they stopped at the store to pick up some supplies. While walking around the store, a new toy caught her eye.

"Mama, can I get that?"
Julia asked excitedly.

PRINCESS SPIN!

HER SPIN

CITY

Julia's mom wouldn't buy her the toy.

"I understand a new toy can be exciting, but let's try to find a way to **appreciate** and **be grateful** for what we have," said her mom, pointing at the toys she brought from home.

NINJA
SPIN!

ERO
PIN!

44

Julia left the store in a bad mood.
She complained the whole way
to the medical clinic.

"I *don't like* my toys at home. My parents never buy me any new toys," Julia grumbled.

IN
GYMNASIUM

Today the medical clinic was set up
at Julia's school for back-to-school
physicals. When Julia walked into the gym,
she noticed a lot of new faces.

"Mama, who are all
these new kids?"
Julia asked as
she looked around
the room.

48

"Some of these kids and their families are refugees. They had to flee* their home in a different country because it wasn't safe. Everything they owned was left there, too. Today we are going to make sure these kids are healthy, so they can go to school."

"I need you to help play with the kids. They are probably very scared and **could use a new friend.**"

"Yes, Mama," said Julia.

*Flee means to leave quickly or urgently

Julia looked around the room and saw a girl about her age. She walked over to her and said, "Hello! What's your name?"

She didn't speak English very well. The little girl looked at her mom who said something to her.

The girl responded, "Yana. My name, Yana."

"Hi, Yana! My name is Julia.
Do you want to play with me?" Julia asked
as she held out one of her toys from home.

Yana's eyes lit up and she nodded her head. The two girls walked over to the play area. Even though they couldn't speak the same language, they still had fun playing together.

"Yana Bitar!"
called Julia's mom.
It was Yana's turn to
see the doctor.

Before Yana left, Julia gave Yana her toy.

"You can have this," said Julia.

"I have enough toys at home."

Yana smiled and she gave Julia a hug.

"Thank you," Yana said as she walked to the doctor.

56

Julia left the clinic that day feeling grateful. She was thankful for her family, her friends, her home and all that she had. **She realized the more she was thankful, the less she complained.**

8am – 3pm

When she got home, Julia picked out toys to donate to the refugee families. She thought a lot about her new friend and hoped she would see Yana at school this year.

THINK & ··· TALK ABOUT IT

Julia's New Friend

Discuss the story...

1. What was Julia's attitude in the store?

2. How did Julia change throughout the story?

3. Describe the people Julia met at the clinic.

4. What is a refugee? Why are they at the clinic?

5. How did Julia feel when she left the clinic that day?

Discuss how to apply the story...

1. What helps you feel grateful?

2. How can you show you are grateful for what you already have?

3. Have you ever moved to a new place? How did you feel?

4. If you had to leave your home and only take one thing, what would you take?

5. When you have more than you need, how can you help others?

FOR PARENTS & MENTORS: *Teaching your child to be grateful and content is a great way to cure complaining. Instead of focusing on what your child doesn't have, redirect your child's attention to what they do have. As a role model, take time out of your day to express what you are thankful for, material and immaterial things, such as food, a safe place to live, family and friends. If your child focuses too much on getting new toys, try giving gifts that are quality time or acts of service.*

In a world plagued with wars and natural disasters, many families flee for their lives and seek safety in other places. Contact local religious organizations or non-profits to see if there are relief efforts near you where your family could help others in need. Follow the QR Code to visit our website for a list of organizations that help others in need. Sending supplies or volunteering can be a great way to serve together as a family and remember what is important in life.

Meet the

mvpkids®

featured in
Cure Complaining™
with their families

FAITH JORDAN

EZEKIEL JORDAN

MRS. JASMINE
JORDAN
"Mom"

HARMONY
JORDAN
Sister

MALIK
JORDAN
Brother

LEO RUSSO

MRS. CLAUDIA RUSSO
"Mom"

JULIA ROJAS

MRS. ISABELLA ROJAS
"Mama"

Faith's No Complaining Game

Faith likes to play a game with her family to make sure the complaining virus doesn't get her family sick! This game could be played at the dinner table, on a road trip, in the morning or whenever is best for your family.

Here's what you do:

- Give everyone five clothespins.
- If someone complains, that person must place one clothespin in the center.
- You can earn clothespins back by reframing that negative thought into something positive.
- If you can't think of a positive way to reframe the thought, someone else has a chance to do it, allowing that person to earn that clothespin.
- At the end, the person with the most clothespins wins!

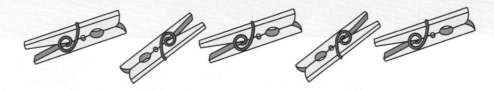

Examples for how to reframe a negative thought into a positive thought:

Negative   **Positive**

Negative		Positive
I don't like broccoli.	-	I'm glad I'm served healthy food!
This is too difficult.	-	This challenge will teach me a lot.
She got a bigger scoop than I did!	-	Look how much I have!

Get creative! Decorate your clothespins and make a stand to hold them. Faith and her family used old tins and paper cups. Look around your house for supplies you want to use. It's really fun and simple!

Grow up with our **mvp**kids®

CELEBRATE!™
Board Books
Ages 0-6

Our **CELEBRATE™** board books for toddlers and preschoolers focus on social, emotional, educational and physical needs. Helpful Teaching Tips are included in each book to equip parents to guide their children deeper into the subject of each book.

help**me**
UNDERSTAND™
Elementary
Ages 6-12

Our **Help Me Understand™** series for elementary readers shares the stories of our MVP Kids® learning to understand and manage a specific emotion. Readers will gain tools to take responsibility for their own emotions and develop healthy relationships.

Help Me Become™ Early Elementary
Ages 4-10

Help your children grow in character by collecting the entire **Help Me Become™** series!

*Our **Help Me Become™** series for early elementary readers tells three short stories in each book of our MVP Kids® inspiring character growth. The stories each conclude with a discussion guide to help the child process the story and apply the concepts.*

Stomp Out Selfishness · Defeat Disobedience · Lock Up Lying · Away With Wastefulness

STAND Up to Bullies · STAND Together Against Bullying · STAND Down, Bullies · Cure Complaining

Phase Out Forgetfulness · Block Bad Sportsmanship · Limit Laziness · Ban Breaking Promises

SOPHIA DAY

www.mvpkids.com

YONG CHEN

LEO RUSSO

FRANKIE RUSSO

JULIA ROJAS

GABBY GONZALEZ

ANNIE JAMES

AANYA PATEL

BLAKE JAMES

SARAH COHEN-GOLDSTEIN

LeBRON MILLER

LUCAS MILLER

FAITH JORDAN

MIRIAM NASSER

EZEKIEL JORDAN

OLIVIA WAGNER

LIAM JOHNSON

Get to know our MVP Kids®!

You will learn and grow with them from book to book. Each MVP Kid® has a personal back story and unique personality, making it easier for kids of all kinds to see themselves and their friends within our books!

www.mvpkids.com

Real MVP Kids

@realMVPkids